QUEST
FOR A
CREDIBLE
MODEL
IN
LENDING EVALUATION

CHARLES K. ADDO

iUniverse, Inc.
Bloomington

Quest for a Credible Model in Lending Evaluation

iUniverse books may be ordered through booksellers or by contacting:

iUniverse
1663 Liberty Drive
Bloomington, IN 47403
www.iuniverse.com
1-800-Authors (1-800-288-4677)

ISBN: 978-1-4502-8961-0 (pbk)
ISBN: 978-1-4502-8962-7 (ebk)

Printed in the United States of America

iUniverse rev. date: 3/19/11

PREFACE

This book examines potential income as an additional independent variable that will complement credit history to predict loan repayment with applicable interest. Lending exposures constitute the most material risk concentrations within banks, and this book contributes to the literature on lending risk management within banks and other lending institutions. Risk management theories have provided emphatic guidelines for risk control and management of banks' loans, yet the results of other studies indicate that the credit evaluation models do not fully explore all available predictors of loan repayment. This deprives the models of total efficiency at predicting loan repayment with applicable interest, and leads to accretion in the nonperforming loans portfolio. It also leads to inequitable credit rationing practices. The resultant effect is a decrease in both investment and consumer spending that stimulates macroeconomic activities.

This book employs the design and administration of original survey instrument to participants. Loan repayment was the criterion, and credit history and potential income were the predictors. Results of the regression were significant, $F(2, 143) = 83.13$, $p < .001$; and credit history and potential income predicted 53.1% of the variance in loan repayment. The findings suggest a policy prescription for lenders: consideration should be given to both credit history and potential income in loan decision making. Lenders may gain useful insight that will help them impose better controls over credit risks.

This book is divided into two parts:

Part I examines the background of the credit evaluation system. It begins with Chapter 1, which provides definitions of key words as used in this book to establish conceptual symmetry with the reader. Next, the chapter provides a rationale for effective credit evaluation system, and then the limitations of credit history as a tool for evaluating credit worthiness. It is then followed by Chapter 2, which identifies the problems with the credit evaluation model and reviews current innovations aimed at solving those problems.

Part II examines potential income as complementary variable to credit history for measuring loan repayment. It starts with chapter 3 with a discussion of the methodology of the study, analysis of data, brief discussion of the concepts of validity and reliability, and provides rationale behind the independently designed survey instrument of the analysis. It is then followed by chapter 4, which provides a discussion of data validation and findings. The book concludes with chapter 5 with a discussion of the impact on social change, actions required to improve upon future studies, and suggestions for future researchers.

ACKNOWLEDGMENTS

Several individuals have contributed to this project. I particularly express my gratitude to Professor Reza G. Hamzaee of Missouri Western State University, USA; and Professor William H. Brent of Howard University in Washington, D.C., USA for their constructive critiques and encouragement. Finally, it is a pleasure to acknowledge the debts that I owe to the many researchers and authors whose work this book has greatly benefited from.

      Charles K. Addo, Ph.D.
      Catholic University College of Ghana
      Faculty of Economics and Business Administration
      Fiapre, Sunyani

      December 2010

CONTENTS

PART I:

BACKGROUND OF THE CREDIT EVALUATION SYSTEM

CHAPTER 1 UNDERSTANDING THE CREDIT EVALUATION SYSTEM

INTRODUCTION

The present society is credit-centered. The enormous advancements that have been made in production technology have generated numerous goods and services in the marketplace. Somehow, those products and services must find ways to consumers through credit sales. The cash-and-carry system of making sales alone, cannot sustain the required level of reduction in inventory that will permit favorable impact on the macro-economy. Sales made through credit have more than ever become a necessary complement to the cash-and-carry system of making sales. But the challenge is that lending exposures constitute the most material risk concentrations for banks and other lending institutions, making credit extension a risky business that is fraught with lagged nonperforming loans. A major requirement that emerged at the proposed Basel II accord[1] recommended that lending institutions reevaluate their exposure to credit risk on an institution-wide basis. The Basel II committee observed that risk concentrations constituted the major problems that banks and lending institutions faced in their efforts to achieve optimal financial stability.

---

1   International Convergence of Capital Measurement and Capital Standards, an organization that promotes greater consistency in the way banks and banking regulators approach risk management across national borders. See also Gleeson, 2004, p. 29.

The role of credit accessibility in the financial security of individuals has been well documented, and some studies have emphasized the importance of educating people about it early on in their lives. For example, one study has advocated for the exposure of younger adults to informed decisions regarding personal financial management, to help them avoid having excessive debt affect their current and future financial security.[2] Another study noted that nearly 31% of college seniors have credit card balances in the range of $3,000 to $7,000, and 9% have balances that exceed $7,000. Many of those young debtors are unable to retire their debt before they graduate and enter the working world. One adverse effect is quite obvious: they may be unable to acquire durable consumer goods on credit when they are out of school.[3]

A very important decision linking durable goods consumption spending and investment behavior is the granting of credit to consumers.[4] Loans to consumers stimulate macroeconomic activities through consumer spending and investments. It enables investors to generate profit-oriented economic activities that directly impact on the level of economic indicators, such as employment. Risk management theories have provided emphatic guidelines for risk control and management of banks' loans; yet the results of other research indicate that the credit evaluation system does not fully explore all available predictors of loan repayment. This makes the credit evaluation system less efficient at predicting loan repayment. Specifically, there is a lack of academic research on the predictive power of potential income on loan payments. Since lending exposures constitute the most material risk concentrations within banks[5], this book will help banks to impose better controls over credit risk.

It has been noted that purposeful control strengthens the management process.[6] Thus, one area where the financial management aspect of business deserves a much closer look is in the area of credit risk management. This involves making sound loan decisions that result in borrowers' repayment of principal with applicable interest. As noted earlier, economic activities would virtually grind to a halt under a regime of total cash-and-carry system by way of excessive inventory buildup. Thus, the concept of credit

2   See Jones, 2005, p. 9-16
3   See Block, 2003
4   See Stanhouse & Sherman, 1968 p. 1263
5   See Gleeson, 2004, p. 29
6   See Schoderbek et al., 1991, p. iv

extension to consumers to pay for goods and services does not only make much economic sense, but also a necessity. To establish borrowers' creditworthiness, lenders frequently turn to borrowers' income and past use of credit to predict loan repayment.[7]

Unfortunately, lenders often consider a shorter-term concept of income, rather than a longer-term concept. They do this because the shorter-term concept offers the benefit of higher predictability. For example, a regular employee paycheck can be said to be more predictable collateral for a loan repayment than potential income from investment in education. In that sense, one may categorize a regular paycheck as shorter-term concept of income due to the shorter time frame that it can be received. Along similar reasoning, potential income from investment in education may be categorized as longer-term concept of income. It is this longer-term notion of income, as expressed in income from investment in education, which constitutes the primary scope and analysis of this book.

While the concept of using *income* as complementary to past use of credit in predicting loan repayment is considered in loan granting decisions,[8] hardly can it be said that similar level of consideration is given to the concept of *potential income* as a factor in predicting loan repayment. For example, factors such as credit consumers' level of education or the impact that certain legal family obligations may have on income are not sufficiently emphasized in the loan-granting decisions. One study[9] buttressed the fact that the credit evaluation model is less than adequate at distinguishing between good and bad credit risk. This is because it does not sufficiently exhaust all available predictors of loan repayment. The general impression is that the credit rationing system is inextricably locked in the concept of credit history, tending to negate the importance of seeing income within the much broader context of human capital investments and potentialities.

Allocation of credit to consumers increases consumer spending and investments, which stimulate macroeconomic activities.[10] Some studies[11], however, suggest there is no efficient credit rationing system that minimizes

---

7   See Volpe & Schenck, 2008.
8   See Avery, 2004; Paroush, 1976; Shenn, 2004; Thompson, 2003; Weston & Brigham, 1993
9   See Tabor & Bowers, 1977
10 See Stanhouse & Sherman, 1979
11 See D'Silva, 2004; Stanhouse & Sherman, 1979; Timmons, 2002

loan default experiences to permit consumer spending and investment to have full stimulating impact on macroeconomic activities. This absence of efficient credit rationing system should naturally raise the issue that the widely used criterion for determining loan repayment, that is, credit history is inadequate.

The idea of categorizing potential income as tangible income was at one point mooted in the US Congress as appraisable for taxation purposes. A bill was introduced in Congress that sought to empower the US tax collection agency, Internal Revenue Service (IRS), to evaluate potential income for tax purposes[12]. If the bill had passed, the IRS could, for example, do any of the following: (1) assess tax liabilities on home owners with vast backyards that could have earned income if cash crops had been planted, or (2) identify citizens with rich relatives and then determine the amount of money a person could have received had the rich relative died and assess tax liabilities. Of course, such tax assessment scenario would have been quite unrealistic. The point, within the scope of this book, is not about the merits of *potential income* as additional source of revenue for the state. Rather, the point is about the notion of why certain proxy variables of potential income, such as educational level, cannot be fully utilized as predictive tools for loan repayment? Of course, the level of education per se is not automatically positively correlated with income, although generally it may be so. After all, it is much more tangible and quantifiable than the legislative proposal referenced above.

THE IMPORTANCE OF CREDIT EVALUATION SYSTEM

Some Definitions

Definitional or conceptual symmetry must be established regarding the meaning of potential income and that of future income. The dictionary[13] defines the word *potential* as "that existing in possibility: capable of development into actuality." It also defines the word *future* as "what is to be; time that is to come; an expectation of advancement or progressive development." Quite obviously, those two words (i.e., potential and future) do not convey exactly the same meaning. Although, they are both suggestive

---

12 See *Free Republic*, p. 1
13 See Webster, 1993

of what is not yet in existence state, they do differ significantly in terms of their probability of occurrence or certainty of an event. Future carries the characteristic of a higher probability of occurrence than potential. Notice that potential is faintly suggestive of remoteness from actualization; whereas, future suggests the expectation of actuality.

This distinction may be better illustrated in the following example: Consider a regular lottery player who is yet to win a prize; where, the remoteness of actual income is indicated here. Because this lottery player is regularly in the game, this player may be considered as having a potential income. This potential income converts into future income only when this lottery player does win a prize; where, the expectation of actual income is indicated here. While actual payout arrangements are being worked out, the lottery player may be considered as having future income, as opposed to potential income.

Likewise, consider an insured person with automobile accident policy that indemnifies against personal injury. This policy remains a potential income, as opposed to future income, until this individual actually sustains physical injury in accident and is determined to be eligible for benefits. At that point of determination, the potential income of the policy converts to future income. Thus, within the scope of this book, the word potential income is distinguished from the word future income. Also, the term potential income is sometimes used interchangeably with income potential.

Why the Need for Effective Bank Loan Evaluation System

Lending exposures constitutes the most material risk concentrations within banks. Studies[14] suggest that the credit evaluation system does not completely consider all available predictors of loan repayment. This condition does not optimize the credit evaluation model for predicting loan repayment. Society of today has evolved into credit orientation, which requires that the issue of loan repayment with applicable interest be examined more closely than ever. It is for this reason that this book examines loan applicant's potential income from both loan officers' and academic researchers' perspectives, in order to determine if it would be a good complementary variable to credit history for predicting loan repayment.

---

14 See Avery, 2004; Frame, Padhi, & Woosley, 2001; Jacobson & Roszbach, 2003; Quinn, 2000

Lenders have traditionally given much prominence to loan applicants' past use of credit to the apparent neglect of potential income. The closest to potential income that are factored into the equation of loan repayment may be future income, as frequently evidenced by lenders verification of loan applicants' sources of income. But from our earlier discussions under definitional symmetry, future income is distinctive from potential income. Yet potential income may just as well be an equally good predictor, if not even a better predictor, of loan repayment.

Empirical literature on the subject of credit rationing and loan repayment point to the fact that the credit evaluation model is not exhaustive, and somehow inefficient, at predicting loan repayment with applicable interest[15]. Thus this book is an attempt to contribute to the academic literature regarding other ways of improving the credit evaluation system. The widely used credit evaluation developer, Fair Isaac Corporation (FICO), whose model is frequently made accessible to lenders through the three main credit-reporting agencies (i.e., Equifax, Experian, and TransUnion) in the U.S. and Canada, does not consider potential income as a factor when evaluating a borrowers' long-term capability and willingness to repay loans. The components of FICO's weights that are considered in evaluating loan applicants' ability to repay loans are as follows[16]:

1. 35% of the score is determined by payment histories of a loan applicant's credit accounts, with recent history weighted a bit more heavily than the distant past.

2. 30% is based upon the total outstanding debt of a loan applicant with all creditors.

3. 15% is produced on the basis of how long a loan applicant has been a credit user, with longer history the better provided a loan applicant has always made timely payments.

4. 10% is comprised of very recent history, based on a loan applicant's efforts to obtain loans or credit lines in the past few months.

---

15 Ibid.
16 See "The Scoring Game," 2004, p. 1.

5. 10% is calculated from the mix of credit a loan applicant holds, including installment loans (like car loans, leases, mortgages, credit cards, etc.)

By this omission, FICO defers the inclusion of other complementary variables to credit history, such as potential income, for loan repayment to individual lenders to decide. FICO provides justification for this deferment under a number of arguments that include:[17]

1. Ease and faster ways of obtaining credit scores streamlines the credit extension decisions.

2. Increased fairness of the credit extension decisions because lenders are able to focus only on facts that are relevant to loan applicants' credit risk, to the total exclusion of personal factors.

3. Past adverse use of credit problems are not significant because they fade away from the report over time.

Examination of those justifications appears to reveal underlying flimsiness. For example, under item number 2, is FICO stating that personal factors in loan evaluation decisions are irrelevant? Or, under item number 3, does FICO realize that even though adverse credit history fades away over time, they stay on long enough to do damage to consumers?

Limitations of Credit History as a Tool for Predicting Loan Repayment

The traditional tool employed by most lenders to predict loan repayment relies to a great extent on credit history. This tool has inherent limitations, which make it less than efficient as loan repayment predictive tool. For example, due to competitive reasons, credit score developers prefer to conceal the specifics that go into their models.[18] This creates a situation whereby, the model is dependent upon information that can only be verified by the developer that produces such model. Thus, the benefits of the scrutiny of 'peer-review' that assures refinement, improvement, and

---

17 For a discussion of this literature see "Understanding Your Credit Score," 2004, p. 2

18 See The scoring game, 2004

quality of concepts is not made optimal. At least one study[19] buttress the fact that the primary concern of developers of credit models is to protect the precise factors that are used in a formula, such as the weights or the coefficients. Given such lack of transparency, the integrity and quality of the models are rendered questionable.

The limitation of credit history as predictor of loan repayment, and the consideration of potential income as complementary predictor of loan repayment are probably reflected in certain actions by the US government. The government, by implication, appears to recognize the inadequacies in credit history. Through the Higher Education Act of 1965,[20] the government implicitly affirms the importance of potential income as a proxy for loan repayment.

For example, in fiscal year 1991, new loans under the Federal Family Educational Loan Program under the Higher Education Amendments of 1992 reached $12.3 billion[21]. The relevant question that is raised here is: What would constitute the primary rationale for the government to guarantee such huge loans to students, many of whom are without significant incomes, and normally considered bad credit risk? Would it not, in effect, constitute admission on the part of the government that such bad credit risk borrowers, without significant present incomes represent some kind of potential income through investment in education? So you see that we have implied evidence that the government has, for about five decades, been recognizing potential income as a variable for loan repayment. Another study[22] also recognizes the limitations that are inherent in the credit evaluation model in assessing risk of default by noting that due consideration should be given to human capital. Human capital does manifest through education, and the connotation with potential income is quite discernible.

19 See Quinn, 2000, p. 3
20 Act that provides grants and subsidized loans for students who would otherwise not qualify for commercial loans.
21 See Eglin, 1993, p. 1.
22 See Paroush, 1976.

Summary

While those reviews may be inconclusive regarding potential income as a complement to credit history for evaluating credit worthiness, they are nonetheless, suggestive of the fact that there is room for improvement in the way loan repayment with applicable interest is evaluated. They point to the fact that over reliance on the traditional credit scoring system without; at least, giving a chance to alternative loan evaluation approaches may be depriving the credit evaluation system of its full beneficial effects.

CHAPTER 2 OVERVIEW OF THE CREDIT EVALUATION MODEL

INTRODUCTION

The goal of this chapter is to synthesize previous works related to the credit evaluation model and system, to buttress the need for complementary variable to credit history for evaluating loan repayment. There are numerous aspects of managerial controls within an organization, but they all essentially point to one main objective: increment to the bottom line or sound financial management. One area of financial management that deserves an in-depth study is that of risk management. Studies[23] have shown that business success and even survival depend to a large extent on the ability of management to structure and implement sound policies on credit risk.

A review of the credit evaluation literature reveals limited studies in the area of potential income being used as complementary variable to credit history for the evaluation of loan repayment. Among those limited studies, significant number appears to identify inadequacies in the credit evaluation system, particularly with the credit-scoring model. These attest to the fact that the credit evaluation model is ineffective. This ineffectiveness of the credit-scoring model is evidenced by the rise in the loan default rate.[24]

---

23 See Friedland, 1999; Guyok, 1998
24 See Timmons, 2002.

The general stream of thinking surrounding the limited literature on potential income as a complementary variable to credit history in determining loan repayment appears to point to the absence of a holistic system. A brief discussion follows:

LACK OF HOLISTIC CREDIT EVALUATION MODEL

Defectiveness of the credit evaluation model

A number of defects have been found to exist in the credit-scoring model, notably arising from the database itself,[25] which is able to capture more efficiently loan applicants past use of credit than it does with loan applicants potential income as indicated by, for example, level of education and other self-improvement activities. Studies from a US national sample of credit reporting agency records suggest a failure to consider local economic environment and individual situations that lead to the development of ineffective credit evaluation models.[26] The credit evaluation model is skewed in favor of credit history, which injures those repairing their credit history or seriously doing so.[27] John Taylor[28] observed that the credit evaluation model does not score on a full range of proxy variables that would measure ability to repay a loan with applicable interest. Taylor further noted that the models can be different and can affect scoring quality, citing the model used by Fannie Mae, Chase Bank, and GE Capital as being dissimilar and unequal.

Steven Hornburg[29] called for the:

> Need to be more vigilant than ever, ensuring that we're not denying access to minorities because we're locking in historical disadvantages [i.e., credit histories] due to discrimination. ...even when we get to the point where we have the best data available for making credit decisions,

---

25 See Avery, 2004.
26 Ibid.
27 See Quinn, 2000
28 An executive of a Washington, DC-based National Community Reinvestment Coalition. See also Quinn, 2000.
29 An executive director of a Washington, DC-based nonprofit organization devoted to ensuring equal access to mortgage markets. See also Quinn, 2000, p. 4.

there will never be a way of having *perfect foresight* [italics added]. The question isn't simply what's the best way of measuring risk and future behavior. The two are linked integrally, but currently there is no way of doing that.

Such characterizations are suggestive of data inadequacy in the credit evaluation model, and a bias towards credit history in credit rationing. Another study[30] observed that the credit rationing system is applied under different standards, which makes it less effective at discriminating the best credit risk customer from the worst customer. These structural defects also do reflect in the credit scoring system as historical deformities and evolutionary infancy that are laden with sample bias[31]. Hendricks[32] noted that the credit evaluation system is in an evolutionary stage, and cannot be characterized as completely fair or unfair. Another study[33] noted that the credit scoring models have inherent sample-selection bias that make them weak and proposed the elimination of this structural bias through estimation of individual default risk to compose a value-at-risk measure of credit risk.

FINDING SOLUTIONS TO THE PROBLEMS IN THE CREDIT-SCORING MODEL

Innovations to the credit evaluation model

Several studies[34] have long identified the problem with the credit evaluation model. Lately, encouraging results have started to emerge from a number of companies, seeking to address the problem with the model. Probably nothing underscores the inadequacies of the traditional credit scoring model, with its over reliance on credit history, more than a recent shift by FICO towards a credit system that will adequately capture long-neglected credit consumers. This shift is testimony to the fact that using credit history

---

30 See Quinn, 2000.

31 See Frame, Padhi, & Woosley, 2001; Jacobson & Roszbach, 2003.

32 Publisher and consultant who frequently testify before the U.S. Congress on protection of consumer credit rights. See also Singletary, 2004.

33 See Jacobson and Roszbach, 2003. This was accomplished through a vast array of data that were obtained from both approved and rejected Swedish loan consumers' credit reports.

34 See Avery, 2004; D'Silva, 2004; Quinn, 2000; Stanhouse & Sherman, 1979; Singletary, 2004; & Timmons, 2002.

exclusively as guarantees for loan repayment is not comprehensive enough of a criterion. In an unprecedented move designed to make available loans to consumers who do not possess credit history, Craig Dillon[35] confessed to the fact that "many people with low or nonexistent credit scores obtained via traditional scoring methods, including our [FICO] credit score, actually are good prospects for loan repayment,"[36] and for that matter are creditworthy. This realization has prompted FICO to introduce a new credit-scoring product that is designed to expand the loan markets in hopes that it will stimulate macroeconomic activities.

According to FICO, "an estimated 160 million Americans have documented credit histories. By comparison, 50 million Americans lack the history required to obtain credit at competitive rates."[37] Dillon predicted that although the traditional credit scoring system is not going to be phased out and will continue to be employed by lenders, in situations where a loan "applicant lacks a credit history, participating credit unions routinely would run the expansion score to identify loan prospects. …[predicting the use of the FICO expansion score to increase] loan approvals [by] as much as 15% to 20%." [38]

First American Corporation[39] took a non-traditional approach to bolstering the creditworthiness of credit consumers who lacked good credit history by developing a credit-scoring system that was targeted toward assisting lenders in determining those without traditional credit history. This idea came about in recognition of the fact that many lenders are shifting towards the notion that the future demand in the credit market was going to be shaped by minorities, who are generally perceived to have poor credit history. At the very least, those efforts imply that all is not well with the credit evaluation model, and may buttress the inadequacies in the model. The prospect of this new scoring system looks very promising in terms of increased volume of credit approvals and consequent improvement in the bottom line for lenders.

---

35 FICO's vice president for product development stationed at Minneapolis.
36 See Dernovsek, 2005, p. 4.
37 Ibid.
38 Ibid.
39 California-based data provider and title insurance company. See also Bergquist, 2005.

Mark Ziegler [40] has come up with a parallel credit scoring option. This option utilizes a software program lending officers employ to increase the volume of lending, and some lenders are already reaping the reward of this innovation. For example, Ziegler noted that one company[41] which extended $21.9 million in automobile purchase loans to prime applicants in 2003 increased this amount to $58.2 million after introducing the program. Simultaneously, it made an additional $18.6 million in mid prime loans, which consisted primarily of borrowers that were bypassed by the traditional scoring system.[42] The goal of those innovations is suggestive of movement towards capturing those loan applicants who exhibit potential capabilities to repay loans with applicable interest, but who lack historical data or good credit history. This lends credence to the inadequacies that are inherent in the credit evaluation model that may very well be filled by potential income.

SUMMARY

In this chapter, a general overview of the limitations of the credit evaluation model was provided. The weaknesses that have been identified with the model were presented. Innovations being made by certain organizations, including the widely used credit developer, FICO, to shore up the weaknesses of the credit evaluation model were also identified. The next chapter will focus on the approach used to access data for this analysis to determine whether potential income is complementary to credit history in predicting loan repayment with applicable interest.

---

40 Senior vice president of the Dallas based Allied Solutions.
41 Albuquerque-based First Financial Credit Union in New Mexico,
42 See Dernovsek, 2005, p. 4.

PART II:

EMPIRICAL ANALYSIS OF POTENTIAL INCOME AND CREDIT HISTORY AS COMPLEMENTARY VARIABLES FOR LOAN REPAYMENT AND CREDITWORTHINESS

CHAPTER 3   METHODOLOGY OF THE STUDY

INTRODUCTION

This chapter presents information about how this analysis was designed, why the use of the quantitative research method, as well as the theoretical model employed is better suited for this analysis. The chapter provides the limitations of the analysis, and discusses three major criteria for achieving sound scientific measurements. Within the contextual framework of those three major criteria, this chapter justifies the rationale behind the development of the survey instrument. This chapter also presents a conservative rule of thumb estimation of the sample size. The categorization of the measuring instruments is specified, as well as the theoretical model that was used to analyze the data collected.

STUDY METHOD

Study Design

The quantitative tradition was employed, which involved a field survey that was targeted at bank loan officers. Using bank loan officers as the target group provided the advantage of having knowledgeable participants who were assumed to have relevant experience in loan granting business. This experience made those participants better than using participants recruited from the general population. For participants from the general population, would have quite likely responded to survey questionnaires, based upon uneducated guesses and intuition that could have adversely impacted on the reliability of the survey responses.

Sample Selection

In selecting the participants, consideration was not given to the geographic location, size of business, type of clients, and business focus of the financial institution. The reason for this is that the criteria that are employed in loan-granting decisions are essentially similar and universal; irrespective of geographic location, size of business, type of clients, and business focus of financial institution. This is because loan decisions are essentially made with one fundamental objective: determination of whether a borrower can repay the principal with applicable interest. Consideration was also not given to the time frame at which a loan decision was made. This is because time, in this case, does not really affect "the nuances of meaning and to changes in nuances of meaning"[43] of the variables.

Sample Size

One conservative rule of thumb for sample size determination is derived from the formula, $n > 50 + 8m$, where: n = sample size, and m = number of predictors.[44]

Theoretically, the number of predictors of loan repayment may be infinite depending upon how many a researcher may come up with. But in this study, the number of predictors was two: credit history and potential income. Those were the predictors of loan repayment with applicable interest, and by extension borrower creditworthiness. Substituting the number of predictors into the above formula yielded the following sample size:

$$n > 50 + 8 \, (2) = 66 \text{ participants.}$$

This sample size was adequate enough for the study, given the benefits of the technical knowledge and experience of the target participants. But to even increase the level of validity and reliability, this study selected a higher number of 146 participants, a number that is more than twice the conservative rule of thumb estimate. Because this sample size far exceeded

---

43   See Cooper & Schindler, 2003, p. 231
44   See Statistics Solutions, 2005, p. 2.

the rule of thumb estimate of 66, extra questionnaires were not deemed necessary to compensate for any drop in the response rate.

Data Collection

The participants were given copies of informed consent document[45] together with the survey questionnaires. The informed consent document informed the participants in detail about their legal rights with regards to participating in the survey. Among the information contained in the consent document were: why they were chosen for the study, background information about the study, the procedures involved in the study, the risks and benefits aspects of the study, assurances of their confidentiality of the responses, and contact information of researcher.

Because the names and identities of participants were not disclosed, this study was considered anonymous. Therefore, a signed informed consent document by both participants and researcher was not necessary. Nevertheless, informed consent document was maintained for the record, even though participants did not belong to a legally protected population, for which reason the informed consent idea was conceived and crafted by legislation. This measure was in keeping with research ethics, as it kept participants aware of their rights, and to make informed decision as to whether to participate or not to participate in the study.

Data Categorization

The data collection was categorized as in Table 1 as follows:

Table 1.

Data Categorization for Credit History, Potential Income, and Loan Repayment

Proxy for Credit History
1. Lateness with monthly loan minimum amount payment.
2. Delinquency and collection of borrower's credit account(s).
3. Total debt of borrower with other creditors.

---

45   See Informed Consent document: Appendix B

4. Number of bankruptcy filing(s) and discharge(s) in court within the past ten years by borrower at time of loan application.

5. Amount of payment in excess of monthly minimum to credit account within last three billing cycles by borrower at time of loan application.

Proxy for Potential Income

1. Annual income of borrower.

2. Dependent family member(s) of borrower.

3. Formal educational level of borrower.

4. Number of alimony payments by borrower.

5. Number of child support payments by borrower.

Proxy for Loan Repayment

1. Total dollar amount of liquid and non-liquid assets of borrower.

2. Age of borrower.

3. Number of co-borrower(s).

4. Job changes of borrower within last two years at time of loan application.

JUSTIFYING CHOICE OF STUDY METHOD

The use of the quantitative research design, using data collected from bank loan officers was most appropriate because the study involved numerical ratings (i.e., Likert scale) that were determined quantitatively through statistic software. Quantitative technique calls for more exact evaluation, as opposed to qualitative techniques that involve subjectivity in evaluations. For example, the number "2" is "2" universally, leaving little or no room, whatsoever, for subjective estimates.

STUDY LIMITATIONS

Ideally, research data that would have most accurately supported scientific reliability of the analysis would have been data collected from the banks or the credit bureaus on credit consumers. But such data were not obtainable for several reasons. Among the reasons for these data not being obtainable were proprietary rights to trade secrecy, the ascendancy of identity theft in recent times, as well as legal constraints that have been imposed on the release of data from files of credit consumers. Regulatory directives and certain court rulings were sending wrong signals to credit agencies regarding the release of credit consumers' information. For example, rulings in favor of the US Federal Trade Commission (FTC) ordering TransUnion credit reporting bureau to stop the sale of consumers' credit report were sending wrong signals to other credit agencies to be wary about releasing data on credit consumers.[46]

DATA ANALYSIS

Credit history, potential income, and loan repayment are three variables that may contain several or even infinite sets of operational definitions. They are continuous variables and a straight line is fundamentally the best approach to model the relationship between those variables.[47] The study used SPSS statistical software to analyze the data, and employed a multiple regression model given by:

$$Y = f(C,P)$$

$$Y = \beta_u + \beta_1 X_1 + \beta_2 X_2 + \ldots + \beta_k X_k + \epsilon$$

Where,

Y = Loan Repayment (i.e., the dependent variable), which is a function, f, on a set of k independent variables (i.e., credit history, C; and potential income, P), X_1, X_2, . . ., X_k, which are considered predictors of Y; and the error term, ϵ.

Multiple regression permits the assessment of the relationship between one dependent variable and several independent variables. It is particularly

---

46 See Appeals Court Upholds FTC Order, 2001
47 See Cooper & Schindler, 2003, p. 580.

suitable for measuring those infinite items in an independent variable whose partial effects or coefficient describes the dependent variable. It is also particularly suitable for prediction. To ensure that a linear regression relationship existed between the dependent variable, Y, and any of the explanatory, independent variables, X_i, the *F*-test was conducted to ascertain the appropriateness of this model for this study using,

Ho: $\beta_1 = \beta_2 = \beta_3 = \ldots \beta_k = 0$

H_1: Not all the β_i (i = 1, . . ., k) are zero

If the null turns out true, there is no existence of a linear relationship between Y and any of the independent variables in the proposed regression model. If the null hypothesis is rejected, it will constitute statistical evidence of the existence of a linear relationship between Y and at least one of the independent variables proposed in the regression equation.[48]

To present a concise determination of the primary focus of the study, a total of 146 participants completed the survey instrument. Participants were asked to respond according to a five-point Likert scale. An *F*-distribution with (*k*, *n*-*k*-1) degrees of freedom[49] was used for testing the null hypothesis, H_0, where k = degrees of freedom of the numerator, n = sample size, and n-k-1 = degrees of freedom of the denominator. [50] Multiple regression was conducted on Credit History and Potential Income predicting Loan Repayment and the variability in Loan Repayment that can be predicted by Potential Income and Credit History.

Validity and Reliability

In theory, questionnaire items that are intended as operational definitions of variables could be infinite, limited only by access to data. In fact, the so-called "ideal" data from the credit bureaus may have their own limitations and shortcomings. For example, a terminally ill loan applicant would be a poor credit risk, because of the high likelihood of death before making a loan repayment. Nevertheless, data pertaining to the health of individuals may not be available for credit bureaus. They may be obtained from health centers, but the process of matching such health data to credit bureau data

---

48 See Aczel & Sounderpandian, 2006, pp. 493-497.
49 See Kanji, 1999, p. 136.
50 See Aczel & Sounderpandian, 2006, p. 352.

of loan applicants could be quite cumbersome and costly. This naturally raises the issue of validity and reliability of data for scientific researches. In this regard, the "ideal" data for research is simply non-existent or not obtainable, for the simple reason that the costs involved would be prohibitive.

Due to the prohibitive costs that may be involved, it became necessary to design independent survey instrument. A good survey instrument for achieving sound measurements in scientific research relies on three major criteria, namely validity, reliability, and practicality. Practicality involves an environment of a wide range of factors such as the economy, convenience, and interpretability.[51] The two most common criteria are validity and reliability, thus it is important that we understand those two words.

Validity "is the extent to which differences found with a measuring tool reflect true differences among participants being tested. …sensitive to all the nuances of meaning in the variable and to changes in nuances of meaning over time."[52] "A measure is reliable to the degree that it supplies consistent results…and is necessary contributor to validity"[53] The distinction between validity and reliability is probably better explained using the bathroom scale analogy that comprised of three scenarios:[54]

1. If the scale known to be accurately calibrated records accurately, then it is both reliable and valid.

2. If the scale consistently overweighs by, for example four pounds, then the scale is reliable but not valid.

3. If the measurement by the scale is erratic or unpredictable from time to time, then it is not reliable and also not valid.

Thus, "if a measurement is not valid, it hardly matters if it is reliable -- because it does not measure what the designer needs to measure in order to solve a research problem." [55]

There are two major varieties of validity: internal validity and external validity. Internal validity poses the question of whether "the conclusions

---

51   See Cooper & Schindler, 2003, p. 231.
52   Ibid.
53   Ibid., 236
54   Ibid.
55   See Cooper & Schindler, 2003, p. 236.

we [researchers] draw about a demonstrated experimental relationship truly imply cause" whereas, external validity raises the question of whether "an observed causal relationship generalize across persons, settings, and times."[56] The above definitions of validity and reliability are not in any way different from those provided by one other researcher,[57] who noted that "Validity determines whether the research *truly measures* [italics added] that which it was intended to measure or how truthful the research results are. In other words, does the research instrument allow you to hit "the bull's eye" of your research object?" The researcher further noted that "the extent to which results are *consistent* [italics added] over time and an accurate representation of the total population under study is referred to as reliability."[58] Thus, it appears that the key characteristic of validity is the concept of *truthfulness* of the measuring instrument, while that of reliability is the concept of *consistency* in the application of the measuring instrument. Guided by the concepts discussed under validity and reliability, rationales for the independently designed survey instrument were provided. However, additional costs required for reformatting and production of tables by the publisher prevented the presentation of the rationale and the survey instrument. They may be available through a request made to the author.

SUMMARY

In chapter 3, we reviewed the approaches used to undertake the study. We reviewed the study design, why a particular design method was favored over others. Data collection methods and data analysis techniques were also discussed. Measures that were taken to protect participants' rights and ensure research ethics were also reviewed. Chapter 3 also provided a discussion of reliability and validity of the measuring instruments, and within that framework, a survey instrument was independently designed.

---

56   Ibid., p. 432.
57   See Joppe, 2006
58   Ibid.

Chapter 4   Data Validation and Findings

Introduction

This chapter presents information on data validation and findings pertaining to the problem of loan defaults. As noted earlier in chapter 1, a number of studies[59] suggest that the credit evaluation model lacks the ability to effectively predict loan repayment. One reason is that it does not exhaust all available predictors of loan repayment. Based on this observation, this study sought to analyze loan applicant's potential income, from both loan officer's and academic researchers' perspectives. The objective was to examine whether using potential income as additional variable to credit history would be a better predictor of loan repayment, and by extension a measure of credit worthiness.

Measures and findings of the study, and a slight adjustment to the sample size are also presented in this chapter. Tables and figures related to the study are also presented to enhance validity of findings. The data collection approach and the justification for the research instruments have been discussed in ample detail in chapter 3. For this reason, attempting to present them here over again would only amount to a repetition of the same rationale and justification behind the survey instrument.

Lenders, of course, consider the income factor as the major item in loan-granting decisions because without income the loan transaction can hardly

---

59 See Avery, 2004; Frame, Padhi, & Woosley, 2001; Jacobson & Roszbach, 2003; Quinn, 2000.

be called a loan transaction. The transaction then may better be called a gift or a giveaway, without any expectation of repayment by the funds recipient. But the limited manner that income is considered leaves much to be desired. Potential income, for example, is least considered, if considered at all, and lenders appear to focus on loan decisions based more on credit history of loan applicants. This constituted the major focus of this analysis. This study investigated whether using loan applicants' potential income in addition to credit history will yield a more reliable indicator of applicants' capability to repay a loan. It involved a testing of the hypothesis:

Ho: A projection of a loan applicant's potential income is not a better predictor of a borrower's likelihood to repay the loan and the applicable interest.

DATA VALIDATION

Descriptive Statistics

SPSS generated the means and standard deviations of the 14 data points. The mean and standard deviation for Credit History over a scale ranging from 1 to 5 was 3.8349 and 0.72810, respectively. That of Potential Income was 4.0216 and 0.69366, respectively. SPSS also generated a mean and standard deviation of 3.5608 and 0.5666, respectively for Loan Repayment.

One of the assumptions of regression for parametric inference is that the errors are "normally distributed with the same variance for each level of the independent variable."[60] Figure 1 shows the normal P-P plot of regression standardized residual. The observed cumulative probability distribution approximates a straight line, which supports the assumption of linearity. Figure 2 presents the scatter plot where the residuals appear normally distributed about the regression line; the assumption of homoscedasticity or the assumption of constant variance was met. In other words, residuals appear random with no pattern, implying no indication of model inadequacy or no heteroscedasticity.[61]

---

60 See Voelker & Orton, 2003, p. 126.
61 See Aczel & Sounderpandian, 2003, pp. 463-464

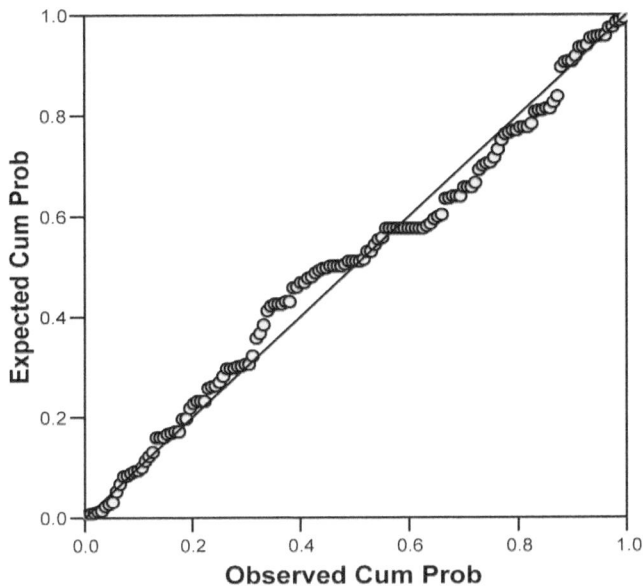

Figure 1. Normal P-P plot of regression standardized residual using loan repayment as the dependent variable.

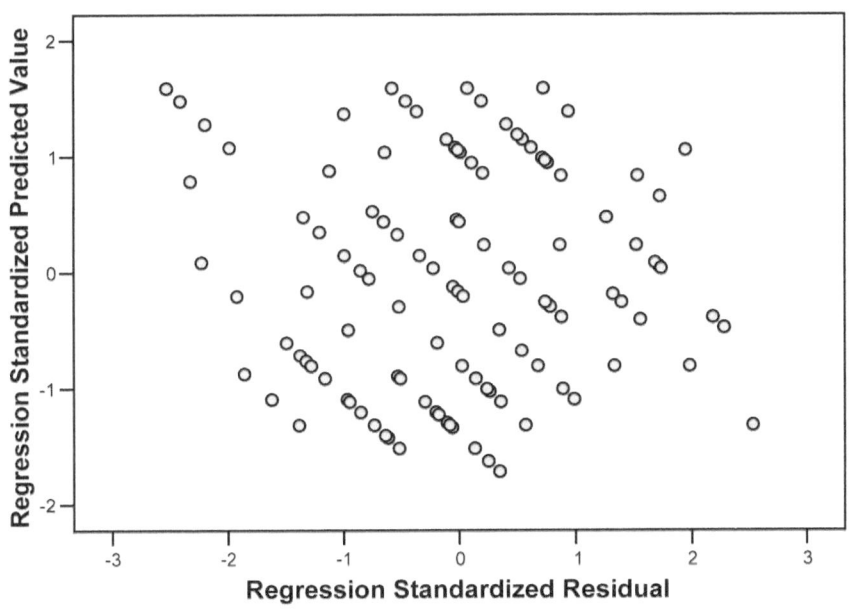

Figure 2. Scatter plot of residuals using loan repayment as the dependent variable.

Charles K. Addo

Multicollinearity

Multicollinearity has a very pervasive effect on every aspect of multiple regression. The reason is that an examination of the relationships between Y and several *Xi* variables produces internal relationships among the *Xi* variables themselves.[62] In other words, some of the operational definitions in an *Xi* variable (i.e., Credit History or Income Potential) may overlap, and appear to imply similar meaning. The ideal *Xi* variables are those that do not correlate with one another; with each variable possessing its own unique information about Y (i.e., Loan Repayment). Table 2 shows the collinearity statistics; where the Variance Inflation Factors (VIFs) of 2.708 for each predictor were relatively small, suggesting that Credit History and Income Potential do not present concern for multicollinearity.

As an example, a VIF of 6 implies that the variance of the regression coefficient estimator is 6 times what it should be, that is, in the absence of collinearity. Multicollinearity "is a matter of extent or degree. It is hard to give a rule of thumb as to how high a correlation may be before multicollinearity has adverse effects on the [a] regression analysis." [63] One study[64] also noted that a VIF of 5 is seen by most researchers as an existence of multicollinearity, although some consider a value of 10 as an existence of multicollinearity.

Table 2.

Collinearity Statistics

	Tolerance	VIF
Credit History	.369	2.708
Potential Income	.369	2.708

Note:
Predictors: Credit History, Potential Income
Criterion: Loan Repayment

Analysis of Variance (ANOVA)

The coefficient of determination, R^2, is a descriptive measure of the strength of the regression relationship, or a measure of how closely the regression

62 See Aczel & Sounderpandian, 2003, p. 555
63 Ibid., 558
64 See Haan, 2002, p. 75

line and the data make a fit.[65] In this case, the value of 0.554 (Table 6) is high; the *F* statistic value of 83.13 is significant. This means there is a good regression relationship, which makes the two independent variables (Credit History and Potential Income) important in the multiple regression equation. The coefficient of determination may take on a value ranging from zero (0) and one (1). A value of zero implies that no regression relationship exists between the predictors or independent variables and the criterion or dependent variable."[66]

Table 3.

Model Summary

Model	*R*	R Square	Adjusted R Square	Std. Error of the Estimate
1	.744	.554	.548	.38234

Note:
Predictors: Potential Income, Credit History.
Criterion: Loan Repayment.

FINDINGS

A total of 146 participants completed the credit rationing survey questionnaires. Three of the responses were discarded for being incomplete. Participants were asked to respond according to a five point Likert scale. Reverse coding was necessary for three of the questionnaire items: Item 5 under Credit History section, Item 1 under Potential Income section, and Item 1 and 3 under Loan Repayment section; during data entry to assure uniformity in the survey instrument. Multiple regression was conducted on Credit History and Potential Income predicting Loan Repayment (criterion). Results of the regression were significant, $F (2, 143) = 83.13$, $p < .001$; and Credit History and Potential Income predicted 53.1% of the variance in Loan Repayment. Beta coefficients are presented in Table 4, where for every one-unit increase in Credit History, Loan Repayment increases by 0.23 units and for every one-unit increase in Potential Income, Loan Repayment increases by 0.41 units. Figure 3 presents the scatter plot for Credit History and Potential Income by Loan Repayment. If a

---

65   See Aczel & Sounderpandian, 2003, p. 457
66   Ibid., p. 459

regression line were inserted from the origin through the data points, it can readily be seen that Potential Income data are very close to the regression line, implying a very good fit. This attests to the significance of Potential Income as a predictive tool for Loan Repayment.

Table 4.

Multiple Regression on Credit History and Potential Income predicting Loan Repayment

Predictors	B	SE	t	Sig.	95% Confidence Interval	
					Lower	Upper
Credit History	.226	.072	3.12	.002	.083	.369
Potential Income	.411	.080	5.12	.001	.252	.569

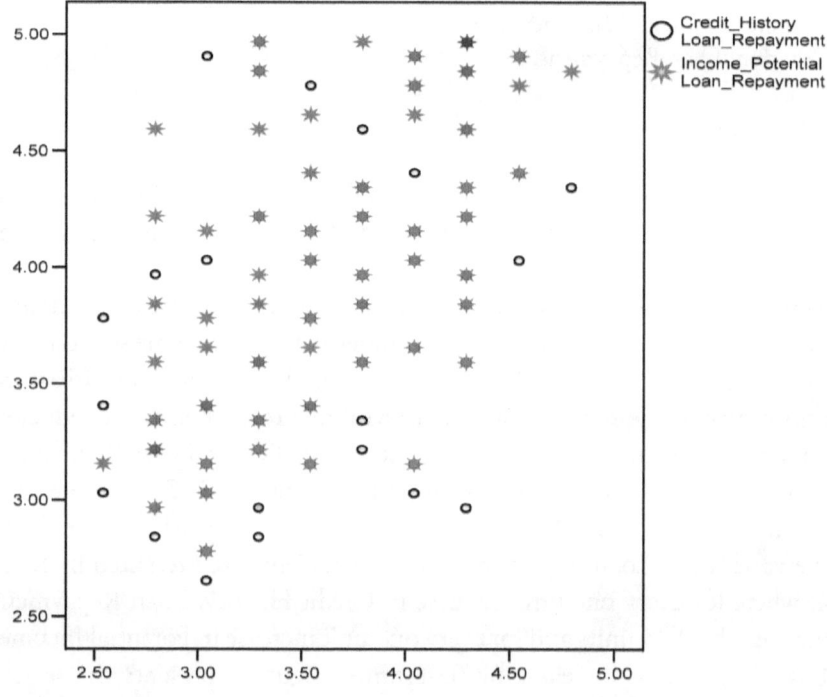

Figure 3. Scatter plot of credit history and potential income by loan repayment.

SUMMARY

Chapter 4 briefly addressed issues pertaining to the research questions. The chapter presented the results of the study, integrating a number of comments on the study. Multiple regression was conducted on Credit History and Potential Income predicting Loan Repayment (criterion). Results of the regression were significant, $F(2, 143) = 83.13$, $p < .001$; and Credit History and Potential Income predicted 53.1% of the variance in Loan Repayment. Beta coefficients were presented in Table 4, where for every one unit increase in Credit History, Loan Repayment increases by 0.23 units and for every one unit increase in Potential Income, Loan Repayment increases by 0.41 units.

Chapter 5 Summary, Conclusions, and Further Research

Introduction

This chapter presents an overview of the necessity and approach for undertaking this investigation. The problem of loan defaults and the ineffectiveness of the credit rationing models cannot be overemphasized. Loan defaults, of course, imply that some borrowers are not creditworthy, which forms one of the corner pillars of this book. As already noted in earlier chapters, some studies[67] suggest that the existing predictors of loan repayment are inadequate to reduce the incidence of loan default. Against this background, this study sought to analyze loan applicant's potential income, from both loan officer's and academic researchers' perspectives. The objective was to examine whether using potential income as additional variable to credit history would be a better predictor of loan repayment. This chapter also focuses on the interpretation of the findings, implications for social change, recommended actions, and recommendation for further studies. Chapter 5 concludes with a note on the beneficial effects that would accrue to society by incorporating potential income as an additional independent variable to credit history to predict loan repayment. Risk management theories have provided emphatic guidelines for risk control and management of banks' loans. Thus the focus of this study was to find out whether using potential income, in addition to credit history, would yield a better predictor of loan repayment. The study used survey data collected from lending officers. SPSS statistical application was used to regress the

67 See Avery, 2004; Frame, Padhi, & Woosley, 2001; Jacobson & Roszbach, 2003; Quinn, 2000)

dependent variable or criterion (Loan Repayment) onto the independent variables or predictors (Credit History and Potential Income). The analysis provided information about variance in the criterion that is accounted for by the predictors as a set. The analysis also provided information about the unique association of each predictor with the dependent variable when all of the other predictors in the regression analysis are statistically controlled (i.e., held constant).

The findings appeared to indicate that both predictors (i.e., potential income and credit history) contribute significantly to loan repayment. Reducing loan default rate acts as great incentive for the release of investment capital, and leads to increased consumer spending. Giving consideration to potential income as a predictor for loan repayment also make homeownership possible for many who would be otherwise judged on their credit history more than their potential incomes. This translates into wealth creation and higher living standards.

MEANING OF THE FINDINGS

The findings suggest that Loan Repayment can be better predicted by both potential income and credit history. Both Potential Income and Credit History can predict a variability of 53.1% in Loan Repayment. The partial coefficient of Potential Income is 99.999% certainty that the results were not due to chance, and that of Credit History is 99.998% certainty that the results were not due to chance (Table 4). Standard error (*SE*) of .072 (Credit History) and .080 (Potential Income) are quite low. This indicates that the scores are tightly fitted around the regression line, which implies a good fit (Table 4). This determination can also be visually observed (Figure 3) where, the scores are closely clustered together, although the regression lines are omitted for the purpose of enhancing legibility of Figure 3.

Table 4 also shows that for every one unit increase in Credit History, Loan Repayment increases by 0.226 units ($\beta = 0.23$) and for every one unit increase in Potential Income, Loan Repayment increases by 0.411 units ($\beta = 0.41$), when each predictor is statistically controlled (i.e., held constant). This emphasizes the fact that Potential Income is a very important predictor of Loan Repayment. Table 4 further shows the t-Test of the significance of the regression coefficient of Loan Repayment on Potential Income, which reinforces the importance of Potential Income as an even more important predictor of Loan Repayment than Credit History (t = 5.12 for Potential Income versus *t* = 3.12 for Credit History). The degree of freedom, F (2, 143), had a value of 83.13 making it statistically significant. The outcome of this study suggests that lenders may have to consider both predictors (i.e., Potential Income and Credit History) as complementary tools for predicting Loan Repayment, rather than over reliance on Credit History.

THE LINK TO SOCIAL CHANGE

Some loan default behavior, and by extension poor creditworthiness of some borrowers, may be traced to the failure of the credit rationing models to consider all predictors of loan repayment, including potential income. This has led to relatively little inflow of investment capital into certain sectors of society. Often, the result has been slowed economic development within such sectors, and this has led to legislative action to correct such inequitable wealth distribution. For example, the Community Reinvestment Act (CRA) of 1977 was enacted to get lenders to re-engineer their lending policies to make them more responsive to the needs of certain low-income groups. Other regulations were also enacted that mandated that lenders invest certain minimum amounts of loan capital in low-income groups.[68] One apparent objective of the CRA was to raise the level of the symbiotic relationship between credit consumers and lenders, in hopes that an economically strong low-income credit consumer base would be able to give back to lenders proportional returns on investment. Another apparent objective was to increase durable goods consumption spending in order to stimulate macroeconomic activities.

ACTION REQUIRED

The primary requirement is for developers of credit evaluation models and lenders to consider the importance of potential income alongside credit history as loan repayment predictive tool, as well as a measure of the creditworthiness of borrowers. This will enable developers to improve upon their credit-scoring model and lenders to eliminate the adverse impacts they suffer when loans go into delinquency. In fact, society as a whole ultimately stands to reap the highest reward if equal consideration is given

---

68 See Van Order & Zorn, 2000, p. 385

to both potential income and credit history as predictors of loan repayment and a gauge for creditworthiness.

Access to more scientifically reliable data was a principal objective of this study. But such access was severely hampered. Among the possible major reasons were legal restrictions. Lenders were quite reluctant in releasing information for research, apparently because of possible legal actions such release of information may entail. Although, one would have expected that the Freedom of Information Law (FOIL) would have reduced the level of reluctance, it was rather the contrary. This naturally raises the question of how useful is the FOIL in scientific research information gathering. The FOIL does not enjoin the release of information for academic research purposes.

This created a secondary requirement, though not necessarily pertaining to this study per se, but its implementation would cast positive effects on academic scientific researches generally. The FOIL may only be applicable at institutional, personal circumstances, and probably investigative journalism purposes. For example, at institutional purpose the New York State banking department may require all banks that operate within New York to submit information about demographics of their loan recipients, for use as sociological analysis tool to ensure compliance with federal fair credit regulations. For personal circumstances purposes for example, it may be used to compel the police to release information about brutalities meted out to a suspect in police custody. For investigative journalism purposes for example, it may be used by journalists to compel a governmental agency to release certain information about unlawful behavior that may not be in the interest of the people for publication.

The action required here is to encourage, through legislative intervention, lending institutions to be forthcoming with certain information that are intended exclusively for academic research purposes. This is not going to be an easy undertaking, given the ascendancy in identity theft. For example, if laws are enacted that would allow credit bureaus to relax access to totally anonymous individual credit information; research of this nature would achieve higher levels of scientific reliability.

One specific proposal for expanding the availability and quality of data for certain academic research purpose could be the establishment of academic research data clearinghouse. Such a clearinghouse, while protecting the identities of credit consumers, would have the legislative power to access real research data from their primary sources, such as the credit bureaus. The clearinghouse would then release the relevant information to researchers after carefully verifying the authenticity through the appropriate Institutional Review Board (IRB). This may be done for a fee to defray some of the administrative costs. Such legislative measures would not only help to advance the cause of scientific research, but also ultimately promote the overall economic wellbeing of society. There is also the requirement for public education focused at increasing the level of awareness of lending institutions. Such education would get lenders to attach much importance to the beneficial effects of releasing data for academic research purposes.

SUGGESTIONS FOR FURTHER STUDY

It is recommended that future studies should endeavor to expand the parameters of the items used as operational definitions for the predictors: the questionnaire items. This means constructing as much questionnaire items as possible to define the predictors (i.e., Potential Income and Credit History) and the criterion (i.e., Loan Repayment). The larger the number of items that define a predictor, the more reliable the study would be. This implies the higher the chances of making accurate prediction about the phenomenon under study. For example, issues about a loan applicant's health may very well be a proxy for potential income that may impact on loan repayment.

In expanding the questionnaire items, caution must be exercised so as to avoid the problem of multicollinearity or having two or more questionnaire items essentially implying the same. Also in striving to expand the parameters, extreme caution must be taken to guard against running into the situation of loading the model with too many parameters. The temptation exists to reason that the more parameters there are in a model, the better will be the model, and therefore the better the statistical model will fit the data. As one study observed, a good statistical model fits the data well but also has as few parameters as possible. The study explained this concept with a mathematical axiom:

Given any two points, we can find a one-dimensional surface, a straight line that [*sic*] will pass through the two points and fit the two points perfectly. [However] Once a third point [i.e., additional parameter] is obtained, it may not lie on the straight line connecting the original two points. Thus, the line-though providing a perfect fit for two points-may be a poor *predictor* of future observations.[69]

CONCLUSION

The empirical evidence supports the fact that in determining loan repayment with applicable interest, potential income does play a complementary role to credit history in a very significant way. Thus policymakers may have to take note when evaluating loan consumers' ability to repay. This will minimize costly default rate, reduce lagged nonperforming loans, encourage increased consumer spending, and stimulate macroeconomic activities.

---

69   See Aczel & Sounderpandian, 2006, p. 491

REFERENCES

Aczel, A. D., & Sounderpandian, J. (2006). *Complete business statistics* (6th ed.). New York: McGraw-Hill/Irwin.

Appeals Court Upholds FTC Order; Trans Union Must Stop Illegal Sales of Consumer Reports to Target Marketers. (2001). Retrieved February 12, 2006, from http://www.ftc.gov/opa/2001/04/ tuappeal.htm.

Avery, R. B. (2004). Consumer credit scoring: Do situational circumstances matter? *Journal of Banking & Finance, 28*(4), 835. Retrieved July 4, 2004, from Business Source Premier database.

Block, S. (2003). Self-control key to managing credit card debt in college. Retrieved July 27, 2006, from Business Source Complete database.

Cooper, D. R., & Schindler, P. S. (2003). *Business research methods* (8th ed.). New York: McGraw-Hill/Irwin, p. 580

D'Silva, V. (2004). Managing credit card risk. *McKinsey Quarterly, 3(*23). Retrieved July 22, 2004, from Business Source Premier database.

Dermovsek, D. (2005). New scoring systems expand loan markets. *Credit Union Executive Newsletter, 31*(5), 4.

Eglin, J. J. (1993). Untangling student loans. *Society, 30*(2), 52. Retrieved July 19, 2006, from Business Source Premier database.

Frame, W. S., Padhi, M., & Woosley, L. (2001, April). The effect of credit scoring on Small business lending in low-and moderate-income areas. *Working paper series* of the *Federal Reserve Bank of Atlanta, USA, 2001*(6). Retrieved July 4, 2004, from Business Source Premier database.

Free Republic. (1999). Retrieved September 29, 2005, from www. freerepublic.com/forum/a3820cc872491.htm.

Friedland, J. (1999). Credit programs for GM, others help fuel growth in Mexican economy. *Wall Street Journal*, Vol. 234, 109. Retrieved July 13, 2006, from Academic Search Premier database.

Gleeson, S. (2004). Inside out. *Lawyer*. AN: 13053440. Academic Search Premier.

Guyok, E. (1998). Peregrine's lack of controls contributed to ruin. *Wall Street Journal*, Vol. 231, *14*. AN: *155622*. Academic Search Premier.

Haan, R. L. (2006). *Absenteeism on Nonprofit Boards: A relationship between board size, attendance policies, training programs, and meeting types*. Unpublished doctoral dissertation, Walden University, Minnesota.

Jacobson, T. & Roszbach, K. (2003, April). Bank lending policy, credit scoring, and value-at-risk. *Journal* of *Banking & Finance, 27*(4), 615. Retrieved on December 01, 2004, from Business Source Premier database.

Jones, J. (2005). College students' knowledge and use of credit. *Financial Counseling & Planning, 16*(2), 9-16.

Joppe, M. (2006). The research process. Retrieved on May 9, 2006 from, www.ryerson.ca/~mjoppe/ResearchProcess/Validity.htm.

Kanji, G. K. (1999). *100 Statistical Tests* (New ed.). Thousand Oaks, CA: SAGE Publications, Inc.

Paroush, J. (1976). The risk effect and investment in human capital. *European Economic Review, 8* (4), 339. Retrieved on July 4, 2004 from Business Source Premier database.

Quinn, L. R. (2000, September). Credit score scrutiny. *Mortgage Banking, 60* (12). Retrieved on January 13, 2005, from Business Source Premier database.

Schoderbek, P. P., Cosier, R. A., & Aplin, J. C. (1991). *Management* (2nd ed.). New York: Harcourt Brace Jovanovich, Inc.

Singletary, M. (2004). Unlocking the mysteries of your credit score. *The Washington Post*. Retrieved July 12, 2004, from www.washingtonpost.com/ac2/wp-dyn/A40418-2004 July 10? language=printer

Stanhouse, B., & Sherman, L. (1979, December). A note on information in the loan Evaluation Process. *Journal of Finance, 34*(5), 1263. Retrieved November 11, 2004, from Business Source Premier database.

Statistics solutions. (2005). Assumptions and considerations for regression. Retrieved December 22, 2005, from www.statisticsolutions.com/Multiple_Regression.htm.

Tabor, J. S., & Bowers, J. S. (1977, Winter). Factors determining the credits worthiness of low-income consumers. *Journal of Consumer Affairs, 11*(2), 44. Retrieved July 11, 2004, from Business Source Premier database.

The scoring game. (2004). *HSH Associates*, Financial Publishers. Retrieved December 31, 2004, from www.hsh.com/pamphlets/aboutfico.html Business Source Premier database.

Timmons, H. (2002, November 25). The cracks in credit scoring. *Business Week*, 3809. Retrieved July 4, 2004, from Business Source Premier database, *Document Reproduction Service No.* 00077135.

Understanding Your Credit Score. (2004). San Rafael: CA, Fair Isaac Corporation. Retrieved August 2004, from www.myfico.com/offers/my FICO_UYC5%20booklet.pdf, p. 2).

Van Order, R. & Zorn, P. (2000). Income, Location and Default: Some Implications for Community Lending. *Real Estate Economics, 28*(3), 385. Retrieved December 2, 2004, from Business Source Premier database.

Volpe, R. P. & Schenck, N. A. (2008). Small business lending environment in emerging economies: A comparison of Brazil and Russia. *Journal of International Business Research, 7*(2), 13-30.

Voelker, D. H., & Orton, P. Z. (1993). *Statistics.* (1st ed.). (J. Borrow, Ed.). Lincoln, NE: Cliffs Notes, Inc., pp. 38, 88, 106.

Merriam-Webster's collegiate dictionary (10th ed.). (1993). Springfield, MA: Merriam- Webster, Incorporated.

APPENDIX A

SAMPLE LETTER OF COOPERATION FROM COMMUNITY RESEARCH PARTNER

Community Research Partner Name
Contact Information

June 1, XXXX

Dear Mr. Xxxxx:

Based on my review of your research proposal, I give permission for you to conduct the study entitled "Xxxxxx xxxxx xxxxxxxx xxxxxxxxx" within this organization. As part of this study, I authorize you to invite members of my organization to participate in your completely anonymous survey. Their participation will be voluntary and at their own discretion. They reserve the right to withdraw from the study at any time if their circumstances change.

I understand that the data collected will remain entirely confidential and may not be provided to anyone outside of the research team.

Sincerely,
Authorization Official
President
Contact Information

APPENDIX B

PARTICIPANT CONSENT FORM

TITLE OF RESEARCH

You are invited to participate in the above referenced research study on *Title of Research*. You were selected as a possible participant due to your knowledge and experience in loan-making decisions. Please read this form and ask any questions you may have before acting on this invitation to be in the study. XXXX from XXX is conducting this study with Institutional Review Board research approval number XXX.

Background Information:

The purpose of this study is to help lenders make more informed decisions when granting loans, so as to minimize loan default experiences, and improve credit worthiness. This will allow lenders to make less risky loans, release more investment capital into the economy, and thus foster increased consumer spending that will stimulate macroeconomic activities.

Procedures:

If you agree to be in this study, you will be asked to assess the relative significance of each of the 14 questions below as a good indicator that a loan applicant will repay a loan. Your response to each question should take about 30 seconds. Thus it will take you 7 minutes to complete the whole 14 questions.

Voluntary Nature of the Study:

Your participation in this study is strictly voluntary. Your decision whether or not to participate will not affect your current or future relations with your employers. If you initially decide to participate, you are still free to withdraw at any time later without affecting those relationships.

Risks and Benefits of Being in the Study:

There are no risks associated with participating in this study and there are no short or long-term benefits to participating in this study.

In the event you experience stress or anxiety during your participation in the study you may terminate your participation at any time. You may refuse to answer any questions you consider invasive or stressful.

Compensation:

There will be no compensation provided for your participation in this study.

Confidentiality:

The records of this study will be kept private. In any report of this study that might be published, the researcher will not include any information that will make it possible to identify you. Research records will be kept in a locked file, and only the researcher will have access to the records.

Contacts and Questions:

The researcher conducting this study is XXXXX. If you have questions later, you may contact the researcher at XXXXX. You will receive a copy of this form from the researcher.

Statement of Consent:

I have read the above information. I have asked questions and received answers. By submitting this survey I am agreeing to participate in this study

INDEX

www.ingramcontent.com/pod-product-compliance
Lightning Source LLC
Chambersburg PA
CBHW021916170526
45157CB00005B/2081